GOD, a Farmer & a Bale of Hay

The True Story of Rich & Fran DeRuyter

GOD, a Farmer & a Bale of Hay

ISBN: 1-931178-58-5

All scripture quotations are taken from
The New King James Version.
Footnotes are added for those who desire to read the
scripture verse in its Biblical context.

Illustrations by Tracie Keifer, 2005

Published by:

Vision Publishing
1520 Main Street – Suite C
Ramona, CA 92065
USA

Dedication

This book is dedicated to Eugene and Darla Smith and Ray Brown. You have made a huge influence on our spiritual walk with the Lord.

Isaiah 43:12 says, "Therefore you are my witnesses," says the Lord, "that I am God." "You-all" are certainly walking, living testimonies on this earth, at this hour, that God is REAL: I see Jesus in You.

Thank you for inspiring us to put into book form this testimony of God's amazing grace in our lives. We appreciate your persuasive encouragement, assuring us that our story is worthy of publication.

Rich and Fran DeRuyter

The Farmer

Introduction

To introduce this book about God, a Farmer, and a Bale of Hay, we find what God can do with a life dedicated to Him. In the farmer/man we find this dedication to be real, strong and true!! God's transforming power is revealed in the farmer, who opened his life up to God Almighty without reservations.

In this farmer/man I have found a friend and brother who is also a man of prayer and faith. Prayer has been, and is the lifeline and guideline of his life. His favorite statement is, "Let us pray about it."

Faith always finds God Almighty involved in the life of the one who surrenders his all to the Master and Savior of mankind!!!

Pastor Delbert Grandstrand
Sunburg, Minnesota

Table Of Contents

Preface

Springtime, the most wonderful season of the year according to many farmers, had arrived in northwestern Iowa. The sun's radiant energy had converted much of the winter's supply of snow into life-giving water. Miracles of new life were springing up everywhere. Nature was painting the countryside green and decorating it with flowers and leaves of many colors. The silver "V' of geese on their northward flights to distant nesting grounds dotted the skies. Little lambs, calves, and foals enjoyed their new freedom as they bounded, leaped, and ran circles around their mothers in the cool of the morning. The daybreak discordant "singing" of various species of farmyard birds, as they prepared to seek food for their new hatchlings, called the farmer to arise from his slumber. Indeed, plants and animals alike were in the business of reproducing their kind.

What an exciting time of the year it was for those who lived in rural America! Since "hope springs eternal," the prayers of many were for summer rains to nourish and mature the new life that spring had supplied in abundance.

Not to be outdone by the creation around them, the DeRuyters added a new sound to the springtime choir. On March 29, 1937, a bawling baby boy was delivered in their farmhouse and welcomed into the family.

On that day, Rich DeRuyter, an unique individual, having a combination of personality traits unlike those of any other person, commenced his journey through life.

Born of Netherlander stock, he was destined, perhaps, to become either a dairy farmer or a flower grower. Rich's father and grandfather were dairy farmers; indeed, the DeRuyters for generations back worked in that noble occupation. Perhaps, the good Lord will allow him to continue that tradition.

The plants in the fields, and the lambs, calves, and foals in the pastures needed the Lord's input to nourish and mature them. Likewise, this little boy required divine help to develop into the man he is today.

This is Rich and Fran's story as told to Eugene Smith and Ray Brown.

Chapter One

A Farmer

Home with Dad, Mom, and Uncle Sam

When I was five years old, my family moved just across the Iowa state border to a farm near Hills, Minnesota. For seven years, I attended public school in that town. Then, my dad bought a farm in Pipestone County close to Ruthton, MN. In 1950, I completed the eighth grade in a country school. Being the top student in my class, I finished my formal education with distinction. Of course, the fact that there was only one student in the class helped a great deal.

My two older brothers were drafted into the US army in the early 1950s during the height of the Korean War. Dad farmed a half section of land in addition to operating a dairy. One man could not accomplish everyday all the tasks that demanded attention; consequently, this very willing fourteen-year-old student turned into a teenage farmer/dairyman rather quickly. During the next seven years, I learned the dairy business, with all its ups and downs, by the hands on method.

At 21 years of age, Uncle Sam required my service in Korea and I was drafted for a two-year stint in the army – fourteen months in Korea. The day I left home,

Dad gave me $60. Greatly impressed with my unexpected wealth, I considered myself a man of means. Never in my lifetime had I seen so much money in one bundle. Upon my discharge from the army, I needed to consider my future; but I had nothing firmly fixed in mind. Perhaps, college in Minneapolis where I could pursue training in electronics would be a good idea.

I noticed an advertisement in the Sioux Falls local paper that offered a two-week job milking cows. I responded to it; the dairyman hired me. My experience working with dairy cows on the family farm must have prepared me well. As the end of my short-term employment period was nearing, the dairyman suggested that I remain on the job and I quickly accepted the offer.

A New Adventure – Family Life

While working on the dairy farm, I met Eleanor, my first wife. Her employment in Sioux Falls, South Dakota and my dairy job nearby meant that we could frequently enjoy each other's company. Eleanor's rather loud, infectious laughter, displaying her pleasant personality, was music to my ears. She was a kind and loving person; I was a shy, quiet farm guy. However, I must have been a smooth talker to boot. We convinced each other that marriage for us was a great idea. In

April 1961, we tied the knot, expecting to live happily forever.

We had just returned home from a short honeymoon. Five days after our marriage, I was working at the dairy farm when I received a phone call from my sister. She told me the devastating news that my dad had a heart attack and passed away. Incredible! My dad dead at 54 years of age! He was far too young to have his life snatched away like that. At first, I couldn't believe what I had heard, and I didn't want to try. Two days before this occurred, I spent the day with him on the farm helping him get ready for the spring fieldwork – cleaning oats for planting and a few other jobs. Now he was gone.

In 1962, Eleanor and I, and my brother and his wife purchased a small farm west of Ruthton, near my parents' farm where my mother still lived. Of course, we left our jobs in South Dakota and became Ruthtonites (or is it Ruthtonians?). My brother and I went into a partnership situation for a time, and we took care of mother's farm as well as our own.

The weather in the summer of 1963 dampened my enthusiasm for farming, temporarily. The often-repeated saying among farmers proved to be true for me: farming is the riskiest business in the world. Hail completely destroyed the second crop of my farming career. To provide the finances that would allow us to remain on the farm and try again next year for that bumper crop (farming operates on "next year time"), I needed a secondary job. I began to drive a bulk milk route, picking up milk from the dairy farms. What was expected to be just a replacement for finances lost to hail, became a decades long enterprise for me.

Eleanor and I started farming with a couple milk cows, a few chickens, and two sows to raise piglets. Our livestock numbers increased rather quickly over the next five years. The demands for water must have become too great for the old well; one morning in 1967, it ceased to provide any water for the livestock or us. We had to dig a new well immediately at a cost of several thousand dollars. You never miss the water until the well runs dry. How true! However, we decided to stay the course and not give in to adversity. I continued to take care of my milk route job, and with Eleanor's help with the dairy, each day's work got done. It seemed like the Lord was merciful to us. We overcame these financial setbacks and we bought out my brother's interest in the farm. Our farming and dairy operations were progressing well.

In 1964 the first little bundle of joy came to dwell in our home. The Lord blessed us with a baby daughter we named Nancy; he repeated that blessing in 1968 when he sent another little daughter, Cathy Jo. He gave

us these two daughters to bring up in the nurture (training) and admonition (counsel) of the Lord. To the best
of our ability at that time, we attempted to raise them
in that manner. Each of them was a great blessing to us
when they were young, and they continue to bless in
their adulthood.

Eleanor and I were in the prime years of our lives.
With our two healthy daughters, we were a happy family, growing in every way – except perhaps, spiritually.

An Unwelcome Intruder

It seems natural for young people to think that they are
invulnerable and that nothing will come along to interfere seriously with their lives. Because both of us had
been taught a strong work ethic when we were
younger, we worked hard tending to the business of
farming. It appeared that we were filled with vim,
vigor, and vitality. According to the old adage "Hard
work never hurt anybody," we had nothing to worry
about.

One day in the spring of 1972, Eleanor informed me
that she had bumped her breast sometime earlier and
that she just discovered a lump there. Without fully
realizing the possible consequences of delayed action
in this matter, she said, "When you get the crop

planted, we'll go to the doctor and have it checked out."

The weather just did not cooperate and the spring planting was on hold. So, I said to Eleanor, "Let's go to the doctor and have him look at this problem." We went to our local doctor who immediately sent us to a specialist in Sioux Falls where bigger and better facilities existed. Tests were done and the results were such that the doctors slated Eleanor for immediate surgery.

I was told that the surgery involved a radical mastectomy because a massive tumor had to be removed. Her condition was so serious that she may not survive the next six months. Obviously, my reaction to this horrifying news indicated the devastation that pierced my heart. The operation lasted from 7:00 am to 1:30 pm. I heard nothing from a doctor or a nurse during that interval of time.

My mind ran wild as it conjured up many frightening outcomes. Two days earlier, I was concerned; now, I'm nearly incapacitated with fear. A state of shock had overcome me. I couldn't remember the floor or room number where Eleanor had stayed overnight. I wandered around in a daze, wondering where I was in the hospital. Finally, a nurse noticed me and asked if I was all right. I said, "I'm OK, but where am I?" She told me I was in the basement. Finally, I got some control over my emotions and drove myself back to the farm. During the seventy-mile drive, I attempted to come to grips with the situation as I heard it that day, but my mind could not accept it.

Eleanor began to take cobalt treatments. Then, chemotherapy became available and the doctor prescribed that new treatment as well. In addition to hundreds of cobalt and chemotherapy treatments over the five years of her illness, she had three surgeries. There were short periods of time during those years when it appeared that the cancer had been arrested, and hope would spring up in our hearts. Hope, that allowed us for a while to dream of happier times again, was always dashed against the rocks of despair. Cancer had returned, but to a different part of her body. Another surgery had to be performed, followed by more treatments.

Our girls were still young and the prospect of losing their mother must have brought terrible torment to them. Eleanor, desperately wanting to see her girls grow up, suffered emotionally, too. During these trying times, Eleanor determined to teach her daughters the duties of the household, preparing them, I suppose, for the sad times ahead. She did a terrific job!

We had no insurance to cover any of the medical expenses that accrued due to Eleanor's illness. As a result, the pile of unpaid medical bills continued to grow with each additional group of treatments. I was a workaholic and already doing all I could do to alleviate the problem. Nothing stresses a workaholic more than the knowledge that he needs to work harder, when he's already doing all he can. There was no possible way I could keep up financially. Although I didn't know how I could manage this stressful time, I just kept doing what I could.

The family in which I grew up attended church regularly; Eleanor, our girls, and I did likewise. We believed we were living by Christian principles. I guess, being an ordinary person, I trusted that all the spiritual teaching I needed would be provided. Somewhere in all the sermons I heard over the years, the simple gospel message must have been preached, but I was unable to search it out. I really never heard the simple gospel.

The Bible says that the heavens declare the glory of God and the firmament shows his handiwork[1]. That I could understand. The countless number of stars that appear in the night sky, hurtling through space at indescribable speed, fascinated me. The big dipper appears the same today as it did when I was a child. However, its stars have been speeding through space in a variety

---

[1] Psalm 19:1

of directions over the decades of my life. They are so far away that they seem not to have moved at all. The moon, our nightlight as the Bible describes it[2], sailing through space on its precise path around our planet, provided amazement and awe. A new calf, nothing more than one tiny fertilized egg cell nine months earlier, is playing beside its mother within an hour of birth. About a week after planting my wheat, I check to see if it has started germinating. Invariably, I find a miracle is taking place. The kernel of wheat itself has split open and died in giving life to a tiny new plant. Surely, God has a purpose for creating everything that exists. I often wonder why God gave me life. What is the purpose of my being here?

A continuation of difficult times often makes one reflect on God and ponder whether He gets involved in our lives. This happened to me. I wondered why this situation came our way to seriously disrupt our family. Why are some so unfortunate and others escape such a trial? I had learned that God is love and that He is actively involved in the things pertaining to the universe. I didn't know if He ever got involved with an individual's life. However, I got bold enough to ask God to help us. We celebrated our 15th wedding anniversary in April 1976. Our families came together for a great an-

---

[2] Psalm 136:7-9

niversary supper. To us, this gathering was a very meaningful occasion.

My sister Gert was truly a ministering "angel in disguise" throughout much of our most difficult times. She came often, and sometimes stayed for weeks to help and to be with the girls. Eleanor was home with us as much as possible. As her condition worsened, someone had to be with her twenty-four hour a day. There were so many situations that caused her a great deal of distress. We had oxygen at her bedside continuously. I slept on the floor beside her bed at night, so I would be readily available if she needed assistance. I hired someone to provide care and comfort during the daytime. Several times I had to put her in the back seat of the car and make a seventy-mile emergency drive to Sioux Falls for hospital care.

Then, one day in August 1977, not knowing this would be our last trip together, I rushed her to the hospital again. Two weeks later, Eleanor passed away. Although her untimely death was not unexpected, her departure from this world left a sorrowful, but thankful family. Naturally, overwhelming sorrow accompanies the loss of a loved one. Naturally, too, sincere thankfulness attends the memory of a life well lived serving her family.

Chapter Two

Building Relationships – A Difficult Task

Life Goes On

On August 19, 1977, a huge black and yellow checker-board sign appeared on my road of life. While it had nothing written on it, I knew its message – end of the road. Five years earlier it was a distant spot; but as Eleanor and I traveled together on the road life dealt us, it continuously grew larger. On this date, it ceased to be a warning and became a reality.

I saw it coming and thought I was prepared for what seemed to be the inevitable outcome, but that was not the case.

Eleanor's passing ushered in a difficult time for me emotionally; however, my greatest concern was for our daughters. How will nine and thirteen year old girls be able to deal with this devastating loss of their mother?

Their welfare became solely my responsibility. This fact worried me greatly because I knew in my heart that I had not been a really good father. As a young father, I was a workaholic and, of course, work was the major priority in my life. There wasn't much time "wasted" playing games and doing things children enjoy.

I loved my girls but I was never able to say to them, "I love you." They never heard that affirmation from me. Without the sure knowledge of my love for them, doubt must have created some confusion in their minds, making their paths ahead much more difficult and frightening.

A short time after Eleanor's death, I met Fran and a friendship developed that brought happiness into both of our lives. Within six months, we were married. Many of our relatives and friends thought that the marriage should have been delayed. My response was simply, "Whether a delay is short or long, Eleanor isn't coming back to us; so let's get on with our lives."

Let's have Fran tell her side of the story in her own words:

Fran's Story

I lived in Ruthton for the early years of my life. Then, in 1964, I left the quiet little town I knew so well and headed for the bustling city of Santa Monica, California. There, I worked for Paper Mate Pen Company for many years.

GOD, a Farmer & a Bale of Hay

My desire to be closer to my sister who was fighting cancer brought me back to Minnesota for a while. I worked in and around the Twin Cities during that period of time. Since I never found a really satisfying job there, I went back to work at Paper Mate in Santa Monica.

I began to detest the ever-increasing traffic situation in Santa Monica and decided that the low-volume traffic of Ruthton would suit me just fine. However, prior to returning there, I went home as often as possible for visits. Upon my arrival at the airport, my sister and brother-in-law always picked me up and we would head for the bar in Ruthton.

On one occasion, as we entered the bar, we noticed two apparently happy, good-looking fellows at a table. Though we were strangers to them, they invited us to sit at their table. While we were enjoying a couple of drinks, Rich and I got somewhat acquainted with each other. Then, we went to the bowling alley for something to eat. Our first lunch together provided a time of pleasant conversation. Soon, Rich and I were meeting for bowling or lunch.

When the time came for me to return to Santa Monica, Rich asked if he could see me when he visited his friends there. Of course, I didn't discourage him.

A short while after returning to California, I decided to move home to Ruthton, so Rich flew out to visit his friends and to help me drive.

Our relationship flourished. Because of my love for animals (and the desire to be with Rich, I admit), I frequently drove out to the farm and helped him milk the cows. Often, after the chores were done, Nancy and Cathy Jo made supper for us. Sometimes, the four of us enjoyed supper in the restaurant. A degree of happiness seemed to be returning to the DeRuyter family.

Wedding plans soon occupied our thoughts and conversations as we worked in the cow barn. Some may consider the barn a very unglamorous setting for such life-changing plans to be finalized. Not having had any formal dates as is customary with most other couples, we quite naturally discussed our future together where we frequently met.

With blessings from Rich's girls and Eleanor's parents, we were married in February 1978.

Discord in the Camp

Our marriage ushered in a short period of happy family life. However, we were to discover that building durable family relationships would be difficult beyond our expectations. Tumultuous times would soon be upon us; fortunately, we had an interval of time in which we all kept our personal emotions under control; unfortunately, none of us had the keys to readily solve the problems that surfaced among us.

Rough Road Ahead

Here is Nancy's description of the girls' lives from her teenage perspective – during their mother's illness and after Fran's marriage to me:

During Mom's five-year illness, it was common for Cathy and me to live short-term with aunts and uncles and we frequently stayed with Mom's parents in Tyler, Minnesota, only seven miles north of our farm. During the school year we often stayed with Dad's brother's family. My cousins also went to the school in Ruthton so we rode the bus to school. Thus, we were able to maintain a fairly stable daily life. We didn't stay away from home for more than two weeks at a time. Most often one of Dad's nieces from that same family would be our live in "help" when we were at home. This routine ceased with Mom's passing.

We no longer had the joy of our cousins living with us. Though toward the end of her life, Mom was in the hospital more than she was home, we missed being with her and talking to her.

After Fran returned from California, she became a part of our lives. Dad was happy and Cathy and I were at home all the time now and enjoyed a more normal life-style. I think I accepted Fran mostly because my little sister was so happy. She was excited about the prospects of having a mom again.

Then, we settled down as a family in the spring of 1978. Emotions started surfacing. First, Fran brought all here personal possessions into our home and started replacing a few items around the house that had always been a part of our everyday world. I distinctly remember our dining room table and chairs being replaced with Fran's. One day we came home from school and all our living room furniture had been replaced with new choices that Fran had made. It was very nice but we had no idea that a furniture change was planned, and therefore, we resented the disappearance of Mom's furniture.

A child's security comes from home surroundings, family relationships, and routines. When changes occur without a child's foreknowledge by communication within the family, the child's security is threatened. My security was threatened from many directions at a very emotional time of a teenage girl's life.

In an attempt to improve our situation, Fran suggested that her adopting us girls might improve our sense of

GOD, a Farmer & a Bale of Hay

belonging and encourage us all to be more concerned about good relationship building. The adoption did occur at an attorney's office in Pipestone, MN. After a couple weeks of relative calm, we found ourselves back traveling in the same old rut that we had been in before the adoption took place.

Expectations regarding chores on the farm and in the house put stress on the relationship between Fran and me. Previously, I was not expected to go to the barn and help with the chores. Now, because of Fran's influence in our lives, we had to do chores morning and night as well as helping out in the house with meals, cleaning and laundry. I do not hold any resentment over the fact that we helped in the barn everyday – on the contrary – I am glad we did. I believe it taught us responsibility and a good work ethic. However, at the time I was a typical teenager and resented having to "work" so hard.

I knew there was a tension between Fran and Dad regarding what I was allowed to do with my friends. She felt that Dad never told us "no." This was often the fuel for arguments between Fran and me. It was not true, he did say "no" sometimes, but to be honest more often he told me "yes." I did not beg for things or for permission that had been denied. I never pushed beyond Dad's first response. Although I never had a curfew as a teenager, I knew that I had better not abuse Dad's trust in me. There were times I did things that I knew made him unhappy and disappointed, but I was never disrespectful and knew to accept the punishment when I got in trouble.

As the years went by ... 1979, 1980, 1981 ... I was not happy regarding the relationship between Fran and me. There were many arguments and unhappy feelings. If I had to attach an emotion to my teenage years (13 to 17), it would be anger. I remember "venting" many times to my best friend.

Reconciliation

Upon graduation from high school, I moved out on my own. We discovered that constructive communication improved considerably when I was not living at home. With the passing of the years, we have made huge strides in our relationship. Fran is truly Mom and she has gained my respect and admiration as time brings us closer together despite the unchangeable difference in our years.

History Repeated

Cathy Jo also became a teenager. O! Happy days were here again! She quite adequately filled Nancy's position as it was vacated. From the perspectives of a child, then a teenager, and finally a mature lady, here are her comments on the DeRuyter family life:

I was excited when Mom came into our lives. As a nine years old girl, I wanted to have a mom again. To live at home on a regular basis brought a sense of stability and real happiness into my life. Our friends and relatives were good to us when we stayed with them, but I needed the security that home life brings to a child. Because I was younger, I probably adjusted to the change more easily than my sister did.

Barn chores and housework were expected of us. At a young age, I had enjoyed going out and helping Dad with the calves, so it was not a big adjustment to go out to do chores. Like every teenager, of course I didn't always have a good attitude about doing chores...but I did them, since that was a part of farm family life.

I do remember having a hard time with the changes in the house after Mom moved in. It was my home, and the changes in my surroundings were unsettling. Why any changes were necessary was a mystery to me. Now as an adult, I can totally understand that she was just making it her home, too.

Mom and I did not always get along, which is probably true for every mother and daughter, but we have become closer as we have grown older. I never take for granted that she is my mom and that God sent her into my life: it is not an accident that she is my mom. I have a stepdaughter of my own now, and I respect her relationship with her mother. I know what it is like not to have a mom and how precious that relationship is.

I was still living at home when we had the first barn revival. I guess I did not think too much of it, because it was something that Dad wanted to do. I trusted that Dad was doing what he thought best and that he would never do anything to harm his family.

Dad started reading the Bible. Soon Mom and Dad stopped smoking and the alcohol was taken out of the house. Since these things had been around my whole life, I could tell something was happening. Mom and Dad began watching an evangelist on TV in the morning before chores. I would lie in bed and listen. At a specific point in the show, I had to get up in order to make it outside to do chores as soon as the preacher was finished. Probably, they didn't think I was listening, but I was.

The actions of parents are more influential sometimes than their words. At the time of the first barn revival, I was 16 years old. I did not get saved at the meetings then, but a couple of months later at the Assembly of God Church in Pipestone, Minnesota, my personal relationship with Jesus began.

GOD, a Farmer & a Bale of Hay

Once Mom and Dad have made a decision, they stand strong and approach it with gusto! This is why God is using them in the Ruthton community. They are well liked and respected and the light of God just shines through them. Their perseverance and dedication through the years are to be commended, as it has not been easy. Many people do not realize that a pastor's job is 24/7/365 (everyday, all day). The phone or the doorbell rings at many odd times of the day and night, and as the flock grows, so do the demands. We all need to pray for our pastors and lift them up to the Lord.

My belief is that when God is involved, there are no mistakes. God puts people in our lives and paths that are supposed to be there; it does not just happen. I believe this is true in my life; I know my mom and husband were both sent to me from God, and I wouldn't have it any different!

Chapter Three

The Farm Financial Crisis

Countrywide Farm Financial Distress

The 1980s brought very difficult times to hardworking farmers and ranchers in our state. All farmers in our area, whether they produced crops such as corn, wheat, soybeans, and/or raised livestock for a living, received unacceptably low prices at the market place. Since most of the farmers here have diversified operations, producing both crops and livestock, they were in serious trouble. Down through the years, when the crop prices were low, the returns from livestock made up for the loss and kept the farmer in business. This was not the case in the 80s. Many times, the farm income was less than the cost of operating the farm. Over a relatively short period of time, this is a fatal formula for any enterprise, and it certainly proved to be so in Minnesota.

Many families had to consider the wisdom of "hanging on" to the farm and the enjoyable lifestyle it offered. Pride, occasionally overruling the farmer's best judgment, forced him to remain actively engaged in farming until all his resources were used up, and he was left with massive debt. Some opted to stay and get off-farm jobs to keep them afloat financially, at least temporarily. Many others who were in serious financial trouble decided, voluntarily or involuntarily, to pack up personal belongings and leave the farm. The difficulties of this world rarely take care of themselves, and many were left with a whole new set of circumstances to confront.

Land prices fell drastically and further aggravated the financial situation farmers were in, especially those who were leaving their farms. Even though land had lost some of its value, farm sales were numerous all over this state where agriculture is a major industry. Of course, the number of acres farmed remained constant, but large corporations were gobbling up the family farms. Not everybody was convinced that this was a good thing for us.

Our communities suffered from the loss of farm population. It is estimated that for every six or seven farm failures one business in the community failed. Job opportunities in the area dwindled, bringing a sense of hopelessness into the lives of those seeking work. A farmer in these dire straits often saw himself as a failure and withdrew from friends and family. Not infrequently, the depression he suffered became so severe that it led to physical illness, thoughts of suicide, and in the worst-case scenario, criminal activity. Our own county knows from first hand experience the truth of this statement.

My Personal Financial Distress

Of course, the 1980s farm crisis affected farmers in many different ways. My problem was a matter of cash flow and the unwillingness of banks to assist farmers in their financial struggles. Let me explain.

We had successful farming and dairy operations throughout the years prior to the arrival of the 80s farm crisis. Our dairy herd, after the expansion of our operation, numbered about one hundred milking cows. Including dry cows and replacement heifers, we had approximately one hundred fifty dairy cattle on the farm.

We worked hard to have a good herd and to keep improving it year by year. Awards for top dairy herd in Pipestone County came our way several years. Individual cows won production awards on various occasions, also.

We borrowed a great deal of money to expand our farming and dairy operations. Our farm and our other assets were collateral security for the loans. An interest rate of 8% was reasonable, but within a year it tripled. Farmers, like me, were in trouble with loans as high as 22% interest.

I had bought new machinery because it made good sense financially to do so. Investment credits permitted me to write off my interest payments; therefore, I paid fewer taxes. But when the interest rates went so high, I couldn't cash flow. I developed a plan to sell new pieces of machinery and buy older ones. If I could get permission to do this, I was prepared to take big losses on this proposed transaction, perhaps as much as $50,000. However, I felt I could stand the loss because I had enough assets in my personal properties and dairy cattle. That would reduce the expenses, so that there was some money left. I couldn't continue to sell my assets to pay the interest. I tried unsuccessfully to explain this to many financial institutions. No bank was willing to give me a new loan and some of them were fairly nasty to us. If I could make this adjustment, I would again cash flow. To me, that made a lot of sense.

Everybody was hurting. The banks were panicking. You see, I could be worth $500,000 today and next week my worth could be less than $100,000. The bottom fell out. Everything I owned wasn't worth much anymore so the loan was no good. What do we do with this situation?

I said to Fran that I was going to try one more bank, and expect God to intervene on our behalf. When I went to this bank they said, "That sounds like a good

GOD, a Farmer & a Bale of Hay

plan, we'll take it." We sold the machinery I intended to sell. By taking my loss, I again cash flowed and was able to start paying down the principal. The plan was working. Looking back at that time in my life, I now know that God opened the door for us by granting us a new loan when no new loans were being given. Praise the Lord!

The Farm Financial Crisis

Chapter Four

The Bale of Hay

The Magazine

How precious are our friends! They help make the journey through life more enjoyable. Whether we meet at a social gathering where many are present, at one of our homes, or on a street corner in town, we readily engage in conversation. If nothing new and exciting has occurred, even a well-told story about the weather can prove interesting. With friends, it seems that the content of conversations, at times, is less significant than the friendship itself. There are occasions, however, when the message is of paramount importance.

After church one Sunday, Jerry Ihnen, a good friend, approached me and said, "Read this magazine Rich. You might enjoy it." Without discussing the contents, he simply placed it in my hand. Knowing that I would be more likely to read it if no pressure were applied, he relied on my curiosity to get the job done. A good friend is always interested in your personal well being. It appeared that Jerry was anxious for me to take the next step on the path of righteousness.

You know the old saying "Curiosity killed the cat." Because of my inquisitive nature, I needed to know what had stirred Jerry to suggest that I read a religious magazine. I did read it and, in this case, curiosity brought life, not death.

A ministry, designed primarily for farming communities, published the magazine; therefore, its presentation of religious material didn't offend this workaholic, roll your own cigarettes kind of man who enjoyed the independent cowboy image.

On the back page, I found a schedule for Henry Vanderbush, a radio preacher. Having become intrigued by the magazine's contents, I thought the radio program could do me no harm. Perhaps, I may find some answers to questions that had concerned me for a long time.

The Radio Program

Since the program was aired at a time when I had to be in my cow barn, I tuned in and turned up the volume so I could hear the radio preacher above the usual barn racket. Soon, listening to this program became a very worthwhile part of my Sunday morning routine.

As the weeks passed, I began to relate to some of the simple, often humorous, down-to-earth illustrations he used to effectively describe important Biblical truths. His Sunday morning messages were becoming important to me because I began to realize that they might have nuggets of truth relevant to my life. My increasing desire to grasp a more in-depth understanding of the preacher's messages caused me to consider carefully many of his statements and the quoted scriptures. While I didn't understand the reason for my increasing involvement with the Bible, the gospel of Jesus Christ was beginning to stir my soul.

My impressions of Christ gained through years of church attendance couldn't peacefully coexist in my mind with the concepts of Christ as taught by this preacher. There was constant conflict between the two. As I persisted in listening to the radio programs, the war in my soul intensified. The preacher declared that Jesus is truly the Christ, the anointed One, the creator and sustainer of everything. He also assured his listeners that Jesus is not only alive but also actively engaged in the lives of people who are presently living on earth.[1] How could that be?

My experience didn't appear to bear witness to such involvement. Moreover, he declared that God's Word has the power to change a person's outlook on life – attitudes, desires, main views, and morals. Evidence of its real effectiveness seemed difficult for me to find. My understanding had been limited to the idea that Je-

---

[1] Hebrews 7:25

sus died on Calvary's cross to cover my sins; then, he went back to heaven so that I could go to be with him there.

This added concept that the living Christ wanted to be involved in my daily life brought bewilderment. Confusion seemed to be my constant companion and I didn't appreciate its company. The preacher told me that I could trust the Word because it's true;[2] he encouraged me to keep reading and to expect the confusion in my mind to be replaced by peace and confidence in the Lord's Word. "For God is not the author of confusion but of peace." [3]

The Word of God, as I had never heard it before, was beginning the long, difficult, but necessary process of reshaping my thinking and, consequently, my life.

An Offering to God

For more than a decade, my life had been filled with stressful situations. Eleanor's five-year struggle with cancer, the second marriage problems, and the farm financial crisis all played havoc with the peaceful lifestyle I had expected. My stress management technique was simple – fill up my days with work. When my

---

[2] John 17:17
[3] 1 Corinthians 14:33

body and mind were occupied with endeavors related to the farm, the difficulties that life threw my way seemed more tolerable for me. A proud man has difficulty admitting that problems exist. I was one of those men and felt that I could handle the everyday troubles that plague a man's life without assistance from anyone. Perhaps, greater attention applied to my family situation would have been more beneficial than anything the extra work accomplished.

In early April 1984, rain, frequent and heavy, had produced mud everywhere. I recall standing in my cow yard among my milk cows – several dozen of them. They and I were ankle deep in an unsavory (absolutely offensive) thick, soupy mess, consisting of mud and an abundance of cow manure. They seemed to be covered from head to hoof with this muck. What a job it would be to get them clean prior to milking! At least for the immediate future, this disheartening sight dampened my enthusiasm for milking cows.

From that elevated vantage point on the edge of my farm, I could see almost all of my cropland. There was water lying in puddles, small and large, everywhere. How discouraged I became as the hope that I would soon be planting the crop faded away.

As I stood there, I began to realize that life seemed to be crumbling out of my control: things just weren't going the way they should go. I knew I had done wrong things and began to feel the guilt that accompanies sin. I didn't know what to do about it. I hoped that God wouldn't let me go to hell if anything should happen to me. I had no assurance in my heart that when I die I would have eternal life in heaven. At this point, the question flicked into my mind: If you die today will you go to heaven or hell? This startled me big time! Perhaps, I had heard the radio preacher ask this very question. Maybe, the Holy Spirit spoke to me. I couldn't respond to the question because I knew neither its source nor the answer.

I once heard this statement: "A person must descend to the bottom of the valley before he can start ascending the other side." I said to myself, "If my present valley is confusion, I must have reached its depth."

Surely, others have suffered the agony of soul that accompanies confusion. Why had no one ever taken the time to discuss these issues with me one-on-one? Where is the peace the Bible declares Jesus left here for us?[4] Lord if you are there to help me, please speak to the winds of life and calm the storm that's raging within me.[5]

---

[4] John 14:27
[5] Mark 4:39

GOD, a Farmer & a Bale of Hay

Right there in the middle of my cow yard, my senses of sight and smell terribly violated, I said, "God, I give up. My life is a mess; my farm is a mess. Look at this farm. I give it to you. You've sure got a mess here. Do whatever you want with it."

In the days that followed, I was a miserable person. My use of tobacco and alcohol increased considerably. Negative, even evil thoughts, came into my mind about things I would never consider doing. The darkness that seemed to be entering into my life disturbed me greatly. What must I do to rid myself of it?

Thanks for the Confusion

One day during this time of internal turmoil, Jerry Ihnen was instrumental again in lifting me one step higher in my spiritual journey. At the time, however, it appeared to me that he just added more confusion.

Jerry, his brother, our wives, and myself often traveled together, as good friends tend to do. In early spring, 1984, we were in Jerry's van going to Marshall for supper. They began discussing the end times, the coming of the Lord, the mark of the beast, and such unsettling spiritual things. Since these terms were not part of my "spiritual terms vocabulary," I sat quietly but far from peacefully, listening to them. The thought "What an unusual conversation for a group of hungry people on their way to a restaurant!" entered my mind. I realized this wasn't a conclusion that a rocket scientist would dwell on for long; but this farmer mulled it over in his mind until the topics of discussion, vital to his spiritual welfare, squeezed out the trivia. At that point, a sense of fear, barely controlled panic, seized my mind.

I knew I wasn't right with the Lord; the radio preacher had convinced me of my perilous situation before God. Jesus, he said, had come to earth to save that which was lost.[6] If I deny Jesus, Jesus will deny me.[7] There is no other name than Jesus' by which I must be saved.[8] That day, as we traveled in the van, God in his mercy convicted me of my sinful condition[9]. Eager that nobody would notice the anxiety that had welled up within me, I tried to look calm, cool, and collected. As soon as we got to the restaurant, I ordered an alcoholic beverage: none of the others did. Attempting to quiet the turmoil within me, I quickly consumed it.

The Bale of Hay

Not long after our journey to Marshall to satisfy our appetites for good fellowship and physical nourish-

---

[6] Matthew 18:11
[7] 2 Timothy 2:12
[8] Acts 4:12
[9] Romans 3:23

ment, I received a spiritual meal that is everlasting. Let me tell you about it.

The morning dairy chores were done, the fields were too wet to work, and the hay land was turning a beautiful green color. The new hay crop would be ready for harvesting in a few weeks. Each spring, time permitting, I had intended to throw the accumulation of leftover hay from the loft of my barn. This I had not done for several years. My dairy cows required good, fresh hay, and I needed to clear out the old bales to make room for the new. I decided that this was the day to accomplish the task that had been low down on my "to-do" list.

Lugging heavy hay bales from the back of the loft and heaving them out the open door at the front required little mental concentration. My mind began wandering from the task at hand and very briefly tried to solve the farm crisis that was presently plaguing the rural communities. A somewhat floundering family situation got a little attention, too. However, my anxiety concerning the conflicting concepts of Christ, my lack of relationship with him, my sinful nature, and my future without Christ could not be quenched. The urgent call from deep within me to deal with my spiritual condition could no longer be denied.

The Bale of Hay

As I was making my way to the loft door with my last bale of hay, a portion of one of the radio preacher's messages flashed into my mind. He told the story of a man who knelt by a bale of hay in his cow barn and received Christ into his life. Seconds before this bale would have landed in the heap with all the others, I found myself kneeling beside it. With tears flowing uncontrollably from my eyes, I uttered, "Lord, I give up. Forgive my sins. Take this confusion from me. Show me the way I should go." [10]

A welcome release from the stress that had overwhelmed my soul for so long bore witness that an amazing happening had occurred. That ordinary bale of hay had become my altar, my meeting place with God.

I discovered that when God decided to intervene directly in my life, He took complete charge of the situation. Without any thought on my part, I found myself kneeling beside the altar and helplessly sobbing before the One who created and reigns over the universe. I cried out for His help; He delivered it swiftly.

My soul, darkened by its conformation to the things and ways of the world, needed a renewing that only the Spirit of Christ could provide. By their cleansing effect on my eyes, the salty tears I shed provided keener

---

[10] Isaiah 48:17

physical sight. The same tears, representing repentance and submission to the Lord, allowed Him to give me enhanced spiritual sight. This insight into the things and ways of Jesus commenced the renewing of my mind so desperately needed. Truly, while kneeling at my altar, I had been given the gift of the Lord's great salvation.

The Bale of Hay

Chapter Five

A Barn Revival? Who's Joking?

Lake Benton Annual Reunion

In April, after my salvation experience beside the bale of hay, the thought came to me that I should get the radio preacher to speak in this area. Everyone needs to hear the message of Christ and His saving grace. The thought persisted for many weeks. Since I'm not an "on the spur of the moment" kind of guy, I like to think about my *good* ideas for a while. Never did it cross my mind that it could be God's idea and that He was persevering with me. I knew that God leads people down the paths of righteousness, but it never occurred to me that He might desire to use me in such a manner as this.

Annually, we had a first cousins reunion on my mother's side. This summer (1984), we had a weekend campout reunion at Lake Benton, fifteen miles from my farm. Saturday evening my sister Gert said that Henry Vanderbush, the radio preacher, lives in this town. The mention of his name surprised me. No one knew that I was a long-time Sunday morning listener to the program; no one knew that I had knelt beside a bale of hay and had become a Christian.

Gert declared, "I'm going to find Henry and ask him to give us a church service tomorrow morning." "Wow, what a great idea!" I thought. They arranged to have a church service at 2 pm Sunday. At the appointed time, Henry and his wife, Ronda, arrived and he gave us a great message that we all enjoyed.

While waiting my turn to introduce myself to Henry, I recalled the following: I used to say rather jokingly, "If you want a preacher to remember you, give him $100 and he'll remember you forever." I sold that old hay I threw out of the hayloft to a neighbor for $100 and sent it to the radio preacher.

Finally, I had my opportunity to introduce myself. The preacher didn't make the connection between the $100 and me and destroyed my theory. Well, he sort of put the two together, after much prompting. I had heard his voice dozens of times before in my cow barn, while I was surrounded by that very peculiar odor that exists there. When we met that day face-to-face, not voice-to-ear, the air seemed unnaturally fresh to me. Some old cowmen are a bit weird, uh?

Following the time of personally meeting those attending the service, Henry and Ronda left our campsite near the Lake Benson beach and returned to their home in town.

Henry's wife left her sunglasses on the picnic table. I said we'd drop them off on our way home to do chores. I went to his door and I thought the man was completely nuts. He said, "Praise the Lord, Praise God, Rich come on in." I said, "No, I can't come in. I've got to go home to milk my cows. Here are your wife's sunglasses that she left on the picnic table."

But he ran passed me, dashed around the corner, grabbed Fran out of the car, and brought her into the house. Henry asked me, "Rich, would you like to see my radio studio? I said, "Ya!" Since this man was the well-known radio preacher that I (and perhaps many thousands of others) had been listening to every Sunday morning, I expected to see a fabulous, immaculate, well-equipped studio. He took me to a clothes closet. There I saw a three-legged stool and a bench supporting his radio equipment.

What a shock! How could this tiny, nondescript radio station effectively transmit the gospel of Christ? How did I know that it had accomplished its purpose for existence? From this tiny transmitter, the gospel of Christ that is the power of God to salvation for everyone who believes,[1] entered my cow barn, bringing conviction of sin into my soul and God's everlasting grace into my life.

---

[1] Romans 1:16

Before we left, Henry asked whether I had ever received Christ. That was the first time I told someone that I knelt beside a bale of hay and asked Christ into my life.

I asked this preacher, "If I find you a place to preach, will you come and preach?"

He replied, "Rich, I'll preach anywhere, I'll come."

The Revival Site Selection

I remember going to town to search out a facility in which we could have a meeting with Henry. At that time, there was no community center in Ruthton. I could not find a building large enough to accommodate an event like I had in mind.

I was still smoking cigarettes and consuming social drinks. The quantity of my drinking had decreased considerably, probably because I was brought up to believe that drinking is wrong. I never considered the possibility that the Lord might be involving me in a weaning process. So, I visited my buddies in the pub as was usual. After the social drinks had been consumed, I left for home. However, not a word concerning my purpose for being in town was divulged to anyone.

Not long after my unsuccessful search in town, Jerry, the same friend who gave me the newsletter in the beginning, said, "Why don't you have the meetings in your shed." I thought, "That's a good idea." Soon my conscience began to trouble me. I worried about using the shed for a Christian meeting.

I remembered that five years prior to this, we built a brand new machine shed about 60 feet x 80 feet. We dedicated the building with a terrific booze party. I bought cases of whiskey and set them on picnic tables. The company that constructed the building, wanting to promote its business, supplied the beef. About one hundred people had roast-barbecued beef dinner and washed it down with booze. The liquor flowed freely; we had a great time. What a celebration!

I decided to see what God would do in a building dedicated to him for a few days. The meeting place was settled.

I called the radio preacher. "I've found you a place to preach."

"Oh, that's wonderful", he exclaimed exuberantly.

"Do you want to visit us some evening and I'll show you the place where you need to preach?"

He replied enthusiastically, "Ronda and I will be pleased to visit your place."

One beautiful September evening, after we had finished milking the cows and doing the other chores, we hitched the team of horses to the stagecoach and set out for a little ride in the countryside (like the city folks go for a car ride to enjoy a summer evening). Soon we noticed a car coming toward us. As it approached our two-horse powered vehicle, to our surprise and great delight, we recognized Henry, his wife, and 10-year old son, Bill. Henry went nuts. "Praise the Lord, Praise the Lord!" he exclaimed. We soon discovered that he loves horses and activities involving them. After a short greeting, Henry's family joined Fran and me on our little country tour.

After treating everybody, including myself, to a pleasant experience in real country living, I was anxious to get at the business that was uppermost in my mind...

"Henry, I want to show you the shed in which we are going to hold the meetings."

"Ah, Rich, let's just go into the house and have coffee, and then we'll see what we can line up," he responded.

"Well, I could show you the shed now before we go in," I suggested, hoping to finalize the meeting place without further delay.

His reply was "We'll just go into the house for now and see if we have some dates available for meetings."

During coffee time, Henry's wife, Ronda, checked their schedule and found that three evenings were available in October. Henry suggested that we hold the meetings right here in the house; it can accommodate 35 or more people.

I said, "No, I think it has to be out in the shed." Henry again declared that there would be plenty of room in the house. How did I know that it had to be held out there? I hadn't a clue; but I knew I must have it in the shed. The strong persuasion I felt within and my persistence resolved this matter in favor of a shed meeting.

I had a vision of putting in an old wagon with some planks on the bunks on which Henry could stand. In a voice indicating that his mind was settled on the issue, he said that neither a platform nor a pulpit was needed.

"I don't want any of that stuff; I'll just stand on the ground" was his concluding comment. My vision to "fancy-up" the surroundings and make it look like we were having a "farm meeting" didn't come to pass.

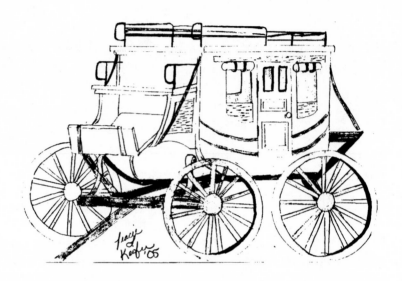

Chapter Six

The First Barn Revival

Where's the Panic Button?

The busy summer season had sped away and ushered in the harvest. In addition to the usual activities, the preparations for the October meetings with Henry Vanderbush demanded my attention. It was early September and our machine shed required a radical facelift. Obviously, the place needed to be made more functional and presentable. Lots of stuff in there needed to be taken out of the building; those things that were to stay must be arranged neatly at the far end of it.

I suspect Henry noticed the shed's condition when he inspected it prior to agreeing to preach there. Why do I say this? One day, Virgil Nielsen drove into my yard and started our conversation by saying, "I understand you are going to have Henry Vanderbush come here to hold meetings. Do you need some help?" After I declared that some assistance would be greatly appreciated, we exchanged the usual good wishes and he left my yard. Soon after this visit, Virgil and friends came and started the cleanup job.

As the dates for the meetings came closer, I realized that I must have more help to put the place in tip-top shape. Among the jobs that I had not done was putting down some new gravel on the shed floor to cover oil patches and whatever else may be there.

One day in the bar in Ruthton, I told the guys there that I would need some help. These were my friends, neighbors, and fellow churchgoers. They had helped me a lot during the five years my first wife suffered with cancer. There was a great deal of traveling to Sioux Falls, South Dakota because of her surgeries and for her treatments. Twice daily the routine dairy responsibilities required attention. In addition, harvest time added a great deal more work to an already overloaded schedule. These are the guys that gave me so much help in my time of stress.

As was typical of my friends, they said, "Rich needs help. Let's go help him. He needs to get that shed cleaned out. Preacher is coming! Preacher is coming!" Some of them may have been having a bit of fun at my expense, but that was the way we dealt with one another. My friends did not let me down. I appreciated their friendship and the assistance they gave me.

Many of them did come out to the first meeting. Most of them didn't respond too well to the message: some said that the preacher talks like we all are going to hell. I thought to myself, they've probably got that right.

As the meeting dates came closer and closer, I began to let peer pressure influence me and fear enter into my thoughts. What are my neighbors going to think? How are my drinking buddies going to treat me? They may chide me saying, "Rich's got religion!"

The fear of rejection and persecution can be a torment to someone who enjoys acceptance. From the situation I allowed myself to get into, no reasonable escape seemed possible.

Friends of this project put up posters everywhere. Newspapers carried Barn Revival advertisements. Henry urged his radio listeners to come to the Barn Meetings and he blabbed my name over the radio continuously. He phoned me and his voice conveyed his excitement about the upcoming meetings. I was wishing I could call them off. If I had found a panic button that could stop this thing dead in its tracks, I would have pushed it.

A couple of times while I was in Ruthton, I met a Christian man right on Main Street. He boisterously blurted out, "I hear the preacher is going out to your place?" I mumbled, "Why don't you shut your big mouth?"

Then, Henry got caught up in the advertisement binge that was running wild in the area. He phoned with this request: "Rich, put that stagecoach at the entrance to your farm and attach a 4 x 8 sheet of plywood to it. Write on the sign:

Farm Revival Meetings
October 10, 11, & 12, 1984

"Henry," I immediately said, "there is no such sign going up on my farm. I will not put up that sign. I don't even know how to spell 'revival'." I hung up on him.

The fear of advertising the preacher's meetings that would take place in my yard almost paralyzed me. Then, attempting to control the irritation that welled up in me, I said to Fran, "Do you know what Henry wants us to do?"

I explained his request and to my dismay she responded, "Well, that's a good idea." Fran didn't know the Lord; she was not saved yet; she thought this was a good idea! With a friend like Fran, who needed an enemy? Fran, being the artistic one of the family and knowing how to spell 'revival,' prepared the sign, and I unceremoniously attached it to the stagecoach.

The First Barn Revival

The night for the first meeting of the Barn Revival arrived. Rain had been falling for several days and our yard was a sea of mud. Rainy wet weather in Minnesota at this time of year usually dampens people's enthusiasm for any outdoor activity; this night was cold and really miserable. I felt a slight sense of rejoicing rising up from within. I began thinking that nobody is going to come to this dumb thing anyway, so why should I be worried about the mud. After all God, it's Your farm now! I gave it to You as I stood in the muck in the cow yard. I remember the lifting of a burden from me as You took possession of it. Now, the farm and also these meetings are Yours, God.

At this point, I found some release from the responsibility of bringing the Barn Revival to this farm home and from the outcome of its being here. Now, God can do with it as He pleases. Still, I could not help saying, "This is my farm. What's happening to my farm?" Fortunately, God is very patient with His own and more than willing to forgive. Whose farm is it? God knows, and He's not about to forget.

To my surprise, people arrived in cars and trucks and parked wherever they could find an empty space large enough for a vehicle to squeeze into. It appeared that the people were anxious to get into the shed and the mud did not stop anyone. I remember seeing some ladies wearing those skimpy shoes that have a strap here and a strap there and large parts missing. They didn't seem to mind the mud and simply walked through the muck as if they were wearing rubber boots. Beyond my wildest dream, people came. When the music started, about one hundred people, young ones, older ones, and some senior citizens were seated on bales of hay, enjoying the sweet aroma of the fresh, well-cured cow fodder.

I was not seated with the others when the service commenced. Before Ronda hit the keys of the old piano, I had manufactured an excuse. It would allow me to come out from behind the workbench where I was partially hidden. Soon, Ronda was beating out the music for a great old hymn of the Church, "I Love To Tell the Story" and the people assembled were lifting the song heavenward. Being a brave soul, I quietly slipped out of the shed, intending to go quickly to the cow barn to look after that (supposed) problem there.

Upon reaching the outside, the Lord laid a blessing upon me that I shall never forget. As the sounding board of a piano multiplies the sound of keys striking the strings, so did the tin of the building amplify the activity that was within it. The praise seemed to saturate the whole atmosphere around our place (Your place, God!). Never had my ears heard worship lifted to the place where it stirred the very soul of man. I shall not forget that glorious experience. Perhaps, ministering angels, sent by God Himself to protect the meeting, joined our earthly choir. God is great and does wondrous thing; He alone is God.[1]

---

[1] Psalm 86:10

After going to the barn to complete my excuse, I returned to the shed to take part in the remainder of the service. I noticed a couple people had their hands lifted up in praise as they sang.

Fran came running to me and said excitedly, "They're here, they're here!"

"Who's here?"

"Those Holy Rollers!" she exclaimed.

"Well, who are the Holy Rollers?"

"They're the strange ones that do weird things," she informed me.

Not wanting to know what she desired me to do with them, I told her we'd just keep watch for a while and see what happens. Of course, their behavior throughout the evening was commendable.

Now, it was time for the radio preacher, Henry Vanderbush, to deliver his sermon. I very quickly understood why he instructed me not to prepare a platform or pulpit for him. He was a fiery preacher who paced back and forth, pointing his finger and directing his eyes at his listeners. I believe if he got careless on my proposed platform, he had a good chance of dropping off the edge. Maybe, he already had that one figured out!

Henry preached a convincing message called "Your Sin Will Find You Out." Frequently, after making an important statement, he put a period on it by declaring a loud "AMEN." Nobody responded with an "Amen" or "Praise the Lord." However, every time he did this, from a little pen at the far end of the shed, came a loud "Baaaaaaa." It was a new born calf offering her comment.

This unexpected response to Henry's first "Amen" brought scattered laughter from the listeners. Each of the following performances by the little heifer caused hilarious laughter throughout the shed. The tension that was present at this first Barn Revival meeting was broken. The Lord knows how to do all things well! He shows His great sense of humor at times to lift bondages off people, enabling them to walk in His blessings. Whether each loud "Amen" caused excitement or fear in her little heart, we shall never know.

What we do know is the same emotions flooded the minds of those assembled. Many became excited as the sermon pierced their hearts, causing them for the first time to see Jesus Christ not only as Savior, but also as a real living person with whom they can have a wonderful relationship. Others felt a little fearful because the style of preaching and worshiping may have been different for them. Church traditions were shattered in that shed on His farm; some found a degree of freedom to begin worshiping in spirit and in truth as King David did – certainly not as exuberantly, but with hands lifted up, they began to praise the Lord.

After finishing his message, Henry gave an altar call. "Consider the bale of hay you are sitting on your altar," he said. Then, he asked the following questions: "Who wants to start following the Lord tonight? Who wants to give his life to Christ? Who wants God in her life? If you want Christ in your life, raise your hand". Hands went up all over the shed.

Because we had coffee and cookies at the back of the shed, Fran was there supervising. Obviously, she had more important business on her mind. When I looked in her direction, I saw that a miracle was taking place. I was blessed because she was receiving the greatest blessing that can be given to mankind. With her eyes closed to shut out distractions and her hands lifted heavenward, Fran was submitting her life to the Lord Jesus, and He was becoming a permanent resident in her heart. What a great day for Fran! Because of Jesus' work on Calvary's cross, He gave her the greatest blessing that any person can receive. She was "born again" by the Spirit of God.

Later that evening, after the people dispersed from our yard, Fran and I had time to discuss the meeting. I was anxious to hear about Fran's experience with the Lord. She said she felt heat flooding her body from the top of her head to the soles of her feet. Her excitement about her new life in Christ could not be contained.

She said to me, "Rich, I have to call my sister."
"Fran, you can't call her now; it's 11 o'clock at night."

"Rich, I have to call her. I must tell her that the Lord is here. She needs to know. I must persuade her to come tomorrow and to bring some cookies."

Fran's desire to see others enter into a personal relationship with Jesus was imparted to her when the Holy Spirit came to live within. This was her first step, under the guidance of the Spirit, toward increasing the Christian church - her first step as an evangelist of the Lord!

God showed us what He could do in a place dedicated to His praise and worship. The booze party held at the building's completion did not hinder God's ability to perform wonders in our midst. God's Spirit fills the space offered to Him. Where the Spirit of the Lord is, there is liberty.[2] Someone must have been praying!

---

[2] 2 Corinthians 3:17

GOD, a Farmer & a Bale of Hay

Hannah Vadnie – An intercessor

All things are accomplished through prayer. Jesus says that we can do nothing (of eternal value) without him; we have not, because we ask not; whatever we ask for in prayer, believing, we will receive. Many believe these things Jesus said about prayer and are actively involved in the prayer ministry. They are persuaded that the effective, fervent prayers of righteous people avail much.[3] Those Christians who dedicate themselves to consistent prayer on behalf of people, communities, and even countries are known as intercessors.

Hannah Vadnie and her prayer partner Laverle Stevens were true intercessors. Hannah lived with her husband in Ruthton; therefore, these ladies understood the spiritual needs of this community. They petitioned the Lord for years concerning the lack of effective spiritual training that would accomplish real lifestyle changes in the people of this area. Hannah knew that a person is what he/she allows the mind to concentrates on. As a man thinks in his heart, so is he,[4] the Bible declares.

If one's thoughts are focused on Christ and his righteousness, one learns to walk the path of righteousness for Jesus' sake. On the other hand, the one who gives undue attention to fleshly demands learns to travel the path of unrighteousness for one's own sake. The for-

---

[3] James 5:16
[4] Proverbs 23:7

mer develops a personal relationship with the living Christ and is not hesitant to express faith in and love for Him. The latter sometimes becomes so self-centered that the heart has little or no room for Christ. A life lived without Jesus often drifts into a sense of hopelessness, depression, and even despair. Such a life is capable of doing terrible things. The fact that this area once suffered several murders within a few years indicated that the services of the Great Physician were urgently needed. Only he could deliver the booster shot that would provide a healthy spiritual climate for the area.

Apparently, when these two prayer partners got together, they often drove throughout the countryside and prayed for the households as they traveled. I later learned that they prayed for my home several times as they passed by. They, through intercessory prayer, beseeched God for a spiritual revival, a time when many would get to know Jesus as Friend, Savior, and Lord of their lives.

To my knowledge, Hannah was the only one in the community who openly expressed her faith in Jesus Christ. Everybody told us to stay away from her. Because of her evangelistic approach to life, she was considered weird, crazy, perhaps even a "brick short of a load." She was such a bad influence in the eyes of most churchgoers that they wanted nothing to do with her.

Perhaps, crazy was a suitable description of her: she truly was crazy for the Lord.

How does one describe the joy that radiated from Hannah's face during the first Barn Revival? Let me try: The broad smile and the look of satisfaction, even triumph, that lights up a boy's face as he pedals the bike he persuaded his parents to buy for him. No, that doesn't do it! Maybe this gets closer: the delight expressed on a little girl's face when she gives her daddy the cookie her hands rolled and patted into shape, and she hears him say, "Thank you sweetheart. Daddy loves *your* cookies!" I think this picture describes what I saw. Hannah, a precious servant of the Lord, witnessed that night the fruit of her persistent intersession. Sensing the Lord saying to her "Well done, my child," her face displayed the overwhelming joy that filled her heart.

Prior to the Barn Revival meetings, I had not met Hannah personally. It was a real pleasure for me to meet her there. In conversation one day after the Barn Revival, Hannah told me that sometime before the meetings she had a vision. She saw a dark cloud hanging over this area. Then, she related joyfully, "When you had the revival meetings at your farm, the cloud lifted." Wow! What an awesome God we serve!

The First Barn Revival

Why My Shed? Why Me, Lord?

When I consider the Creator of everything that exists, whose name is called *Wonderful, Counselor, Mighty God, Everlasting Father, Prince of Peace,*[5] I am amazed that He used my humble shed to bless the several hundred spiritually hungry souls who assembled there. One might think that the *Everlasting Father* would have chosen the biggest and grandest church in the area in which to perform His "wondrous things." Perhaps, He is not as interested in the grandeur of a building as He is in its availability for the Holy Spirit's use.

One might also believe that the *Mighty God* would have selected the pastor having the largest congregation in the area to make the necessary preparations for the revival meetings. I am astonished He allowed me to have a part in arranging these meetings in which many souls were added to the Kingdom of God on earth.

I am surprised that this ordinary farmer, with no formal education beyond the eighth grade, was privileged to have a part in birthing the concept of Barn Revivals, starting here on my farm. (Forgive me Lord; I temporarily forgot: It's YOUR farm.) Why was I given the part that I played? I don't know. Why was David, the least likely of Jesse's eight sons, chosen by God him-

---

[5] Isaiah 9:6

self to be king of Israel?[6] I don't know that either. However, it's comforting to know that God said of David, "He is a man after my own heart." [7]

---

[6] 1Samuel 16:11-13

[7] Acts 13:22

The First Barn Revival

Chapter Seven

The Second Barn Revival

Divine Intervention

Fran and I were still basking in the excitement of the first Barn Revival, and marveling at the wondrous things the Lord did in our midst. Pondering the mysteries of God and not fully understanding any, we constantly thanked and praised Him for intervening in our lives, bringing to many, healing for the body, soul, and spirit.

Several times we thought about our involvement in God's planning for these meetings; but more often, we considered the parts played by others as they lived their daily lives. No one knew that God would use some specific statement or event in his/her life to further the divine plan to bring salvation to lost souls.

While God placed in our hearts the desire for evangelical meetings in the shed, He had already attended to the details necessary for the accomplishment of his purpose – heart-changing revival. A quick scanning of the story shows that the Director of this project used several people, my cow barn and shed, and a bale of hay. Each person and prop had to be in the right place and at the correct time. Why did my friend Jerry give me that magazine with Henry's radio schedule on its back cover? God knew that I needed the edification that only the Scriptures can provide, because the gospel of Christ is the power of God to salvation for everyone who believes. Also, he provided the radio preacher, the teacher I needed to assist me in the learning process. Why did Jerry, wonderfully used in the planning stages, suggest we use the shed as our meeting place?

God was initiating the concept of Barn Revivals. He needed a place where people, searching for the Lord but unlikely to enter into a church, could assemble and hear the way of salvation. Why had that hay been left in the loft of my barn for three years? The Lord needed a bale of hay there on that April morning, because He knew I would use it as an altar to kneel beside, as I sought forgiveness of my sins and a new life in Christ.

Henry, well trained in all aspects of evangelism, was a major contributor to the success of the Barn Revivals. We wondered why he had achieved so much success as an evangelist. Was it his knowledge of the Word of God? Was it his teaching skill? Was it his concern for lost souls? Yes, to all three questions. However, as our relationship developed, we discovered these important aspects of his personality. He's a great encourager. From the beginning, when I was reluctant to take the next step, he gave me the confidence to move forward with the Lord. Henry's also an "up and at it" kind of guy who is always anxious to suggest ways to take a project in the right direction as quickly as possible. "Let's get at it and enjoy the adventure" may be an endearing quality of his life.

How can I draw a picture to help you see my friend as I see him? Some may think that one shouldn't attempt to compare the personality of a man with that of a horse; but both Henry and I have been sufficiently associated with horses to know that there are personality traits common to both.

The typical thoroughbred is a discerning creature. Like man, he can distinguish between a normal day and one of adventure. As soon as his groom appears in the morning, he puts his analytical skills to work. If the early morning activities are routine, then, the remainder of the day is likely to be uneventful. If, however, his early morning workout on the track is skipped, he anticipates the upcoming race. The challenge of another new adventure gives birth to a restlessness that intensifies with the passing hours. Finally, in the warm up ring (paddock), he hears the shout "Jockeys up." At this point walking becomes painfully slow. He, restrained by the lead pony, arrives at the track prancing and "tugging at the bit."

Henry, like the thoroughbred, has developed skills of discernment relating to the physical world in which we live. However, man through experience and the guidance of God's Spirit can discern spiritual things as well. He noticed that the spiritual climate of the area, though at a higher level than prior to the Barn Revival, was reaching a new normal. While the Ruthton area was still feasting on the previous spiritual meal, Henry continued to advertise Barn Revivals on his radio program. He told the farmers who lived within range of his voice that God would use any barn or shed they offered for revival purposes. Soon, farmers living in various states began to call him about meetings in their buildings. Henry's spirit rejoiced as he allowed himself to dream of the various barn revivals that may become reality in the near future.

The excitement of past glories no longer stirred him. Henry, having heard the call "Set your dates," was anxious to arrange for the '85 edition of the Barn Revival. He arrived at our place with a spring in his step and "tugging at the bit" to schedule a new adventure.

"Rich," he said, "We must set up dates for the Revival on your farm. Many, from far and wide, want to schedule meetings. I've got to sit down with you and see when the farmers around here aren't so busy. We can't have it in planting season or at harvest time. When is there a lull in farming activity?"

"Henry, we'll have to schedule the meetings between hayings. By the middle of June, we should be done with the first crop of hay. That'll be the best time to have the Barn Revival here. That settles it. Sometime near the middle of June 1985 is Revival time."

The excitement generated by the first Barn Revival had not died down, as one might have expected. Instead, the enthusiasm for the Holy Spirit's involvement in human affairs increased steadily. People's curiosity and sincere interest prompted many from states all around us to ask, "What's happening in Ruthton?" This little village in Southwestern Minnesota became the hub of a newly kindled spiritual flame that was spreading like wild fire in all directions. Although, some local advertising, word of mouth, and the radio program had spread the news of the upcoming second Barn Revival, it became obvious that the Lord had attached the label "Divine Intervention" to this project.

The Light Bulb Sermonette

One day prior to the commencement of the Second Barn Revival, Henry arrived at the farm and went immediately to the shed where the meetings would take place. It appeared that his interest was centered on inspecting its readiness for God's ministry to the people who would be attending.

The Second Barn Revival

I knew that Henry was obsessed with clean glass windows and lights on his car, but not until this occasion did I realize that his concern extended to light bulbs as well. His glance upward at the string of lights in the middle of the shed brought forth the exclamation, "Rich, have you never cleaned those light bulbs? We must do it right now."

I didn't have a long enough "free standing" ladder that would let him reach the light bulbs. Not wanting to squelch his desire for cleanliness, I had to find a solution to the problem. Being a "make do with what I have" kind of guy, I brought in the tractor with the bucket on the front – the one I had used that morning to clean the manure out of the cow barn. Of course the bucket had never been cleaned. Why clean it just to get it mucked up again? I wondered if Henry would consider the stinky bucket more offensive than the dirty light bulbs and abandon the project. Not letting a little adversity dissuade him, he jumped into the bucket and demanded that I hoist him twenty feet heavenward. What a servant of the Lord!

Having completely removed the dirt from the exterior surfaces of all the light bulbs, he declared that the light had chased away the darkness and had filled the entire shed. Unable to resist an opportunity to preach, he delivered a tiny sermonette, drawing this analogy: The bulbs' filaments generated light but it was unable to penetrate the glass surfaces because of the filth there; consequently, the shed remained in relative darkness. However, when the dirt was removed, the light readily escaped through the glass, illuminating the shed's interior. The gospel of Christ produces a different kind of light (righteousness) but it is unable to enter into the soul of man because of the sin that is harbored there; consequently, man remains in darkness, walking the paths of unrighteousness and pursuing worldly things. When the Holy Spirit is able to convict man of his sin, and to convince him to accept the salvation provided by Jesus on the cross, then the light of the gospel can begin filling up man's soul with a desire for righteous living.

The Second Barn Revival

This time we had four evening meetings (June 6-9, 1985) and a closing meeting on Sunday afternoon. People from states all around us and as far away as Oklahoma and California came to see what this Barn Revival excitement was all about. Fifteen hundred people attended over the five-day period.

One evening on their way to the meeting, Henry, Ronda and their son, Bill, were driving along the gravel county road leading to my farm. Suddenly the wildly excited boy yelled out, "Look! Look! Dad, an airplane is landing behind us! To the amazement of all three occupants of the car, an airplane really did land behind them and taxied into my yard. Considerable disbelief registered on the faces of those already assembled as they witnessed this very unusual arrival.

When the pilot was asked how he knew where the Revival Meetings were being held, he responded, "No problem, from the air I could see strings of vehicles coming from all directions merging on this farmyard. I just found a stretch of road between two vehicles long enough to land the plane and followed the traffic."

There were vehicles parked everywhere: in my yard, on the driveway, and along the county road. Many went home after the meetings; the rest stayed and slept in their vehicles, in the barn, or in the shed on bales of hay that had been used as chairs earlier. You never knew where you'd find somebody sleeping overnight.

Showers of Blessings

We saw miraculous healings and deliverances from drugs and alcohol. People dead spiritually came alive spiritually. Many were filled with the Spirit of God. Let me tell you about one healing I shall always remember. A man, bald on one side of his head, said that part of his brain had been damaged by drugs and did not function properly. He felt that if he came to this barn meeting at Ruthton he would be healed. He said a big man had to pray for him. There was a minister there that night who was a very large man. He prayed and the man, totally healed, started to leap and yell. He tipped his cap and threw it upward into the rafters of the building. He shouted, "I'm healed. I'm healed. I'm healed." What a miraculous healing! Jesus said he came to give life abundantly[1] and he did just that for this man and many others.

I received an unexpected but wonderful personal blessing, too. After the meetings, a lady came up to me and said, "You don't know me, but your first wife, Eleanor, and I were school friends many years ago. When she was ill, I visited her in the Sioux Falls hospital. After we discussed the Lord Jesus and our need to receive forgiveness of sins, I asked her if she would like to invite the Lord into her life. She expressed her desire to be saved for all eternity; together, we called on the Lord, bidding Him to enter into her heart as Savior and Lord."

I stood amazed and somewhat shocked at this wonderful revelation of God's absolute faithfulness to all who will believe in His Son, Jesus.

---

[1] John 10:10

Reflections

After the excitement of this amazing meeting dwindled, and those who were staying had found "comfortable" places to sleep, I felt a sense of sorrowing. Why did I not know the gospel of Christ years ago? How different our lives might have been! My mind would not rest and began recalling past circumstances in my life. In the following paragraphs, I shall attempt to relate some of the things I pondered before sleep finally came that night.

I remembered that on occasions before my salvation experience, I had wondered if there really was a heaven and whether Eleanor was there. The lady (I call her an "angel"), whom I had not seen before and have not seen since, brought closure to that concern. God's love, grace, and mercy required that my "angel" lady be at Eleanor's bedside to show her the way of salvation. Because our heavenly Father is not willing that any should perish but that all should come to repentance,[2] He arranged the date, time, and place for this significant occasion to become reality. Truly, she was God's messenger sent to facilitate Eleanor's salvation experience and to bring peace into my heart.

---

[2] 2 Peter 3:9

After commencing the development of my relationship with Jesus Christ in 1984, I began to realize the immense importance of accepting the Lord into my life. Now, I see even more clearly the wonderful benefits my soul has obtained. The author of that great hymn Amazing Grace declared, "I once was blind, but now I see." I, too, was blind concerning the things of the Spirit, but now, I am beginning to see further into the mystery of life – life as the Lord intended it to be: life that cannot be lived successfully without Jesus' indwelling presence. Let me try to explain:

My human spirit had been dormant since birth. No real spiritual growth had taken place in the previous decades of my life. In spite of a religious upbringing, involving regular church attendance and training in the usual principles of correct living, I had not developed an interest in the things that are precious to the Lord. Like a leafless tree, in survival mode during the long wintertime, unknowingly awaits the spring sunshine, I existed physically, longing for a springtime surprise of some sort.

God granted me the surprise I didn't know I desired. At the time of salvation, Jesus, in the person of the Holy Spirit, came to dwell within me, God's new creation. The Holy Spirit became my guide, my comforter, and my teacher. With His help, I began to understand the Scriptures as I read them. Jesus declares in the New

Testament that He is the way, the truth, and the **life**.[3] The Holy Spirit certainly brought the words of the Bible to **life** for me. Since the gospel of Christ is the power of God to salvation for everyone who believes, I delighted in the fact that the glorious gospel had been taught in my shed that evening.

I recalled the momentous occasion when Jesus, God's Son, died. Three wooden crosses stood atop Mount Calvary. In the center, Christendom's famous "Old Rugged Cross" was firmly planted. With huge spikes through His hands and feet to secure Him, Jesus, God's beloved Son, was lifted up from the earth and suspended there. A criminal was hanging from each of the other crosses.

One of them mocked Jesus saying, "If you are the Christ, save Yourself and us." The other one begged Jesus saying, "Lord, remember me when you come into Your kingdom."

Then Jesus, suffering the agony of the cruel cross, but still full of love and mercy, declared, "Assuredly, I say to you, today you will be with Me in Paradise."[4] It's interesting that the criminal who begged Jesus to remember him was given eternal life instantly. That

---

[3] John 14:6

[4] Luke 23:43

thought must be welcome to many of us who have let most of life's precious time slip away before accepting Christ's offer of salvation.

Jesus said, "And I, if I be lifted up from the earth, will draw all peoples to Myself." [5] That is exactly what He has been doing since He shed His blood for the salvation of all who will believe in Him.

Without the center cross on Mount Calvary to which Jesus was nailed and on which His divine blood was shed, my soul would have been lost for eternity. When I ponder the mystery of it all and the mercy He has given me, my soul and all that is within me blesses the Lord.[6]

Oh, give thanks to the Lord, for He is good! For His mercy endures forever.[7] Isn't it wonderful to know that our Father's mercy is for now and eternity?

The Ordination of a Cow Barn Preacher

With the number of Barn Revivals springing up in states all around us, I decided that we should have a special ordination suitable for a cow barn preacher. Henry Vanderbush was rushing around preaching at

---

[5] John 12:32
[6] Psalm 103:1
[7] Psalm 106:1

barn revivals: he was the one to be ordained. We took him out to the barn, sat him down on a three-legged stool under a cow that had been lying down with her tail in the gutter. He was instructed to keep milking until she swatted him in the face with her tail. To the merriment of all spectators, she obliged with a direct blow to the mouth. His ordination completed, Henry leaped up and declared, "I haven't tasted anything like that since the introduction of diet pop." Only an experienced cowman preacher would know how to check for the degree of humility necessary for ordination. Henry passed my test with flying colors!

Someone asked me if I had ever been ordained into the cow barn ministry. I quickly said, "Yes, many years ago and many times since."

The annual Barn Revivals continued at my place until I sold my farm in 1988: about seven hundred people attended each year to receive the Lord's blessing.

The Farm Sale

About 6:00 o'clock one morning, a man drove into my place and asked me if my farm was for sale and, if so, what price I had on it. I had neither advertised the farm for sale nor suggested to anyone that I might be interested in doing so. However, since this early morning visit was so unexpected and unusual, Fran and I sought advice from the Lord concerning this matter. After a third inquiry in one week, Fran said that we should pay attention to this situation. Perhaps the Lord is giving us direction again.

The Scripture states, "Where there is no counsel, the people fall; but in the multitude of counselors there is safety."[8] I had applied this concept several times before when an important decision had to be made. Therefore, continuing the practice, I asked several experienced pastors for advice. The consensus seemed to be, "Set a price on your farm. If the prospective buyer is willing to pay it, sell it to him." He was willing to pay; I agreed to sell. My life as a farmer was nearing an end.

Our sale was a bit different from the usual farm auction. This one started with prayer seeking His blessings on the people and the entire proceedings. On the top of the hayshed, I had secured a large plywood sign saying, "Don't curse the Man who died for you." The deck on our house proudly displayed this bold statement "Jesus saves." As I walked through the crowd, I heard comments like "This guy must be religious."

As I reflect upon that day, I am amazed at the spiritual progress the Lord had produced in my life. Four years prior to the sale, I was almost debilitated with fear pre-

---

[8] Proverbs 11:14

ceding that glorious first Barn Revival. Fear of man and what he might think about or say to me nearly overwhelmed me. Before the auction, my sincere desire was to lift up the name of Jesus and to request no disrespect of His wonderful name. What a change! What a great God we serve!

We farmers are familiar with an old adage "You can't make a silk purse out of a sow's ear." That's true, but don't issue a challenge to God, for He just might prove that proverb untrue. He has been smoothing my rough edges, changing my heart's desires, and placing in me a yearning to walk the pathway of righteousness for His name's sake.[9] It hurts at times, but keep at it Lord!

---

[9] Psalm 23:3

Chapter Eight

Weekly Home Bible Study

No Bible Study in My Home

After the First Revival meetings, Henry suggested that I start a weekly Bible Study in my home. Recognizing Henry's attempt to take me out of my comfort zone by launching me into a more extensive ministry, I offered my usual response, without hesitation, "No, I'm not going to have any Bible Study in my home."

The experienced evangelist's eyes saw many things that happened; he understood their significance; he knew the next step to take. I didn't really understand it all.

"But Rich, you need to follow up. Many people have become interested in the Lord. Think about the things He's done at the meetings. They must be taught the Word of God. You can't leave them without a teacher. That's like leaving sheep without a shepherd. You know what sheep do when left alone - they get lost. Don't they?"

"Henry, I'm a cowman not a shepherd, but I think you're right – they get lost."

Shortly after my conversation with Henry, I met my friend, Virgil Nielson, who had known Henry for a long time. I thought this was a good chance to check out the Bible Study thing, hoping he would agree with me. I said to him, "Henry thinks I should have a Bible Study in my home. I'm not going to have that. Nobody will come anyway." (I remember saying the same thing before the Revival Meetings.)

Virgil responded, "Oh, don't you worry; they'll come."

I didn't know if I wanted a Bible Study in my home. But, we did start one. I don't seem to be the one who makes decisions anymore. It appears that I have lost control over what happens on my farm. Could it have anything to do with that time I stood in the middle of my cow yard, ankle deep in muck? Oh! I wonder if God has taken over…?

Every Monday evening people came to our house for Bible Study. Henry, a man of the Word, a man of God, was our regular teacher. We were fascinated with his messages in which he related humorous incidents to illustrate Bible truths. Because he was a captivating type of person, people loved him and wanted to be where he was preaching. On the occasions when Henry was otherwise occupied, we invited a pastor or a teacher of the Word to instruct us. People came from far and wide to hear the Word of God.

As the numbers grew, drastic change occurred in our house. We had to remove walls to accommodate up to ninety people who were hungry for the Lord. Every week God, the creator and miracle worker, did some astonishing thing: someone accepted Christ as Savior, someone got healed, or someone received deliverance. We all watched with amazement as He worked His wonders in people's lives. A sovereign move of God was taking place in our home (excuse me Lord, Your home). These weekly studies laid the foundation for our personal relationships with God and the development of our Christian lifestyle.

The Whiskey on the Rocks Party

Fran and I still smoked three packs of cigarettes a day between us; I hadn't yet entertained the thought of giving up my cigarettes or my whiskey. Within weeks after the studies started, we both developed a sense of uneasiness about certain aspects of our lives.

Let me draw this picture. When you sit on an unpadded chair for a long period of time, you begin to feel some discomfort and your body starts to fidget around a bit. You decide that you need to do something about the situation. Likewise, when a Christian continues doing something that is wrong, the mind becomes restless and the sense of anxiety increases. This is what I call conviction. It's the Lord's way of letting you know that

He does not approve and that a change in your lifestyle would bring Him pleasure.

When conviction has done its work, you become willing to submit to the Lord's desire for your life; you realize it's in your best interest. This happened to us.

Our tradition was to sit down at the kitchen table and have coffee and a snack before we started the 5 o'clock milking. One day (traditions are hard to break) we were doing the usual thing in the late afternoon. I decided that this is the day to tell Fran what is about to happen. This was somewhat difficult for me because I consider myself to be a "man of my word." I knew that if I told her I was stopping the smoking habit today, I would have to break the addiction without fail.

So I blurted out, "Fran, I believe that the Lord wants me to stop smoking." As if relieved to have the occasion to tell of her conviction, Fran responded saying that she believes the Lord wants her to quit, too. Knowing that the Lord was the One who brought this conviction upon us, I suggested that we pray, asking the Lord's help in this matter. Then, we decided to have one last cigarette together. We puffed so vigorously on those cigarettes that the whole room was filled with smoke.

Now, we laugh about this "dumb" thing we did. Was it really such a dumb thing to do? As a period at the end of a sentence says, "That's it, no more," so did that smoke filled room also declare, "That's it, no more." My smoking habit was broken immediately and I've never had another puff on a cigarette. Fran's deliverance from the habit was almost as quickly accomplished. Does the Lord answer prayer? He certainly does!

Jesus declared that he would never leave us or forsake us. I have accepted all of God's Word as the truth, but this particular nugget of truth has impressed me more than some of the other great promises. Since the day I tuned the radio in my cow barn to Henry Vanderbush's program, He has never left me – indeed, He has never left me alone. The Hound of Heaven (Holy Spirit) has been sniffing at my heels, perhaps ready to nip a little, if I fail to keep moving in God's direction for my life. At first, I did not understand, but now I do. Because of His great love, He wants the best for me.

It appears that God really enjoys delivering people from their bondages. Now, it's the whiskey that must go. My "to go" list is definitely not like His. Whiskey is near the bottom of my mine.

The enclosed porch on my house was eight feet wide. My liquor was stored in a three-shelf cupboard the full width of the porch. I had all kinds of liquor in there. Someone asked me if I could make a "Bloody Mary."

My quick response was, "Ya! that's easy. I can make that and any thing else you might want."

Now, the One who wants the best for me is saying, "Rich, you really should quit drinking whiskey." By now, I am beginning to realize that when the Lord speaks, the best path to travel is obedience. So I quit drinking whiskey. This caused little or no stress because my cupboard contained lots of wine and the refrigerator in the basement was full of beer. For a short while, I continued consuming both.

You guessed it correctly. Next, I felt convicted about drinking wine. It became part of the forbidden contents of my cupboard. By then I figured out the sequence of events and, knowing the next step in the weaning process, I frequently visited the refrigerator in the basement and guzzled a beer or two.

I thought of John the Baptist who realized that as Jesus' ministry on earth increased, his ministry must decrease. Knowing that the Holy Spirit was producing more of Jesus' nature in me, I acknowledged that my desires and selfish ways must decrease. The Lord gently prepared me to give up the bottle willingly. Long before the supply of beer was consumed, I heard the expected word and said, "That's it, no more."

My once precious liquor supply now sat in the cupboard, treasured by no one. I didn't need it and I didn't use it. Why keep it! I decided that I would throw a Whiskey on the Rocks party. I backed the old pickup to the porch door and loaded every bottle of beer, wine, and the once cherished whiskey into it. I drove by the cow barn and a grove of trees and stopped at an old silage pit that had been filled with rocks.

The party began! I picked up an unopened bottle of the once prized whiskey and heaved it against a large rock. My soul rejoiced with loud laughter as I heard the sound of breaking glass and saw the "fire water" (booze) splashing in all directions. Praise God! Praise the Lord, I yelled. With every bottle that met its dismal end smashed against the rocks, I exclaimed, Praise God! Praise the Lord! What a Whiskey on the Rocks party! Just the Lord and I attended. I enjoyed His company; I think He enjoyed mine.

After my hay bale experience in the loft and Christ's coming into my life, I still went to the bar and drank with the guys. I would look around and see unhappiness written on the faces of many of my drinking pals. I began to notice their lifestyles and to realize that the way we live influences our happiness and our state of mind. Most of my buddies appeared to have one problem or another. Actually, one might say that half of them were divorced and the other half wished they were.

After I stopped drinking, I didn't want to be in the bar anymore. The atmosphere was distasteful and depressing, so I quit going there. Then, the ridicule started.[1] My friends came to me saying that I won't drink with them anymore because I think I'm too good for them.

I believe the Lord told me how to make good come out of a bad situation. I said to them, "No, you're wrong. I was so bad that I needed help. That's how bad a person I was. I'm not too good for you. In fact, I believe you're a much better person than I am because you don't say you need any help, but I needed Christ as my Savior. I was defeated and destroyed: He pulled me out of the pit. He was my deliverer. Everything I was doing was leading to destruction of my body and finally my soul would be lost. I solved my problem by accepting Jesus into my life and becoming a Christian, a member of the family of God."

My Bible – No Longer a Shelf Sitter

My hunger for the Word of God increased steadily. The desire to read my Bible was so great that I took it everywhere I went. Whenever I sat down to eat or rest for a few minutes, I attended to both my physical and my spiritual needs.

---

[1] John 15:20

GOD, a Farmer & a Bale of Hay

My Bible traveled with me in my tractor cab when I went to the field. I read it as I worked my land. From it I had learned the importance of prayer. When I finished seeding a field, I would get off the tractor, stand behind the seeder and pray, giving the whole thing to God, because I had done all I could do. I couldn't make it grow: God had to do that. My faith was in Him for the harvest.

That same Bible had been in the barn countless times and from its pages the cows heard the Word of God. What a weird thing to do! While the cows received no benefit, I became more familiar with the gospel of Christ. Even my reading aloud skills improved as I continued with this apparent foolishness. Perhaps, a desire to minister the Word was born in my cow barn.

Throughout the day, when not concentrating on something requiring close attention, I found my thoughts turning toward the things of God. The Holy Spirit who lives within me was renewing my mind. By changing my thought patterns, He caused my way of thinking to imitate that of Jesus. Jesus said that He came to earth to do the will of God. Increasingly, doing the will of God became the desire for my life.

I sensed a growing yearning in my heart to enter the ministry, and for a while, I entertained the thought of attending Bible School. What an unbelievable change this shy, quiet man was undergoing! The man, who had refused every opportunity to speak in front of people, had become willing to testify of the Lord's goodness. My immediate family, relatives, friends, and even I marveled at the change. Now, because of the growing number of Barn Revivals, I have opportunities to speak in many churches, barns and sheds.

To my mind, that represents a changed life, a true conversion. Henry had been watching my spiritual development and, once declared to me, "There's a place for people like you; that place is heaven." Hallelujah!

Chapter Nine

God's Miracle Bat

In the spring of 1986, two years after my salvation, a severe trial came my way and decided to hang around and interfere with my farming activities. I developed a hip problem that brought constant pain and a limp into my life. Whether I stood, sat, or lay down, I had no relief from pain. It's likely a temporary problem, I thought, but that was not to be. The pain intensified to the point that I could not tolerate putting much weight on my leg. I practically dragged it along as I walked.

I knew that the Lord Jesus healed many when He walked this earth. The scripture declares, "Jesus Christ is the same yesterday, today, and forever."[1] It was not difficult for me to believe that my pain was happening in the "today" era. Since He has not changed, He heals today. What more proof do I need than the marvelous healings I witnessed in the '85 Barn Revival? So I decided that I'm going to pray and be healed.

Every church service, I went up to the front, whether or not the pastor gave an altar call. I remained there until I received prayer for healing. After a while, the chitchat began. There goes Rich limping up to the altar again.

---

[1] Hebrews 13:8

He must not have enough faith for healing. There must be something wrong with his life. He must have some sin with which he needs to deal. Rich needs to confess that he is healed and stand in faith.

I knew that healing hadn't taken place. The limp and the pain were still my unwanted companions. I had no intention to lie about it. Negative thoughts like "Maybe they're right" began to creep into my thinking and I had to kick them out of my mind immediately. I tried not to let this prattle bother me. Convinced that God would heal me, I continued to drag myself to the altar for prayer. Jesus says that we have not, because we ask not. So, I decided to keep on asking until I receive my blessing.

Various people and preachers began recommending different healing ministries. Many prayed for my healing with no apparent results. The numerous hands that were laid on me almost wore the hair off my head. Through it all, I kept thinking that God would heal this condition.

Because my problem kept getting worse rather than better, we rented out the farmland; but we kept the hay land, since we intended to continue operating the dairy. With Fran and the girls' help, we would handle it.

When I went out to hay, I had to crawl to the swather and pull myself up on it. At the end of the day, the process was reversed: I had to crawl back to the house.

Certainly, God has given wonderful healing skills to medical doctors. Through this difficult time, I was under a doctor's care. He determined that there was some deterioration of the hip socket, but a pinched nerve was causing the severe pain. Not knowing how to deal with the situation, he sent me to a specialist in Sioux Falls, South Dakota. There, I had X-rays of my hips and awaited further information from the specialist.

One day, I pulled myself up onto my old 4020 tractor and headed out to work. I pondered about my physical problem and wondered why I was not healed. Certainly, I had been persistent in asking for it. I thought about the finger pointing, accusation, and persecution that had been coming my way and realized that I was sick of it all.

In the middle of the field, because of the severe pain, I carefully got down from the tractor and gingerly knelt before the Lord and prayed. "Lord," I said, "I'm really sick of this. They say, 'He believes in that healing stuff and look at him.' I don't know what to do. I give up."

I got off my knees and up on the seat of my tractor. Immediately the thought came to my mind, "How did I do that?" I got off the tractor and back up again. There was no pain and my leg worked perfectly. There hasn't been any pain in that hip since. While the doctors were considering what they should do, the Lord stepped up to the plate with His miracle bat and hit a homerun for me. Hallelujah! What a great God we serve!

Why did I receive healing in the middle of my field instead of in a church, while a preacher was praying for me? I simply do not know. If God intended to heal me in that manner, he had a multitude of opportunities to do so. He's the potter; I'm just the clay.[2] He neither needs nor seeks my assistance in His decision-making.

As a pastor who lays hands on the sick and prays for their recovery, I have been questioned many times about different aspects of healing. The only thing I know for sure is that I cannot heal anybody. The Lord is the One who gives the signs and wonders. He decides if, when, and under what circumstances a healing will take place.

---

[2] Isaiah 64:8

Chapter Ten

The Country Church

The weekly Home Bible Studies in our home generated great excitement in our hearts and produced anticipation for the next meeting. The Lord never failed to bless us in some way. Fran and I were so hungry for the things of the Lord that we began attending the Sunday evening service at various churches. We delighted in attending churches where the people believed that Jesus is alive and actively involved in their lives. An Assemblies of God congregation in our area fit that description, so we frequently visited there.

We witnessed people receiving the Baptism of the Holy Spirit, speaking and singing in other tongues, and the prophetic word in operation. These happenings were strange to us, but we readily accepted them since we had experienced the Holy Spirit at work at our Monday meetings.

Perhaps, the Lord was preparing us for another comfort zone shake-up that He knew was just around the corner.

Some members of the Bible Study group decided that Sunday morning services would be great for their families. We had a meeting concerning this suggestion and, thinking that this would develop into a church fellowship, I was not long in telling those assembled that I would not be their leader.

One of the men spoke up and said to me, "Rich, you've got to stop saying 'no' to everything. You've got to do what you've got to do."

I thought, "He's never spoken to me that way before. Maybe I should listen to him. Perhaps, the Hound of Heaven is nipping at my heels again."

I promised to consider the request. I didn't know if I wanted to go that direction in ministry. Because of the incredible increase in Barn Revivals, I was preaching or giving my testimony at many of them. My desire for evangelism, ministry to those who don't know Jesus Christ as Savior, was beginning to burn within me.

I contacted my friend and mentor, Delbert Grandstrand. This was my usual approach to situations dealing with the spiritual aspects of life. He is a longtime pastor and a great student of the Word of God. This was his advice to me: "Rich, attempt to stay completely away from ministry for a while. If you just cannot remove it from your life, then go into it with all your heart."

I accepted Delbert's advice and soon discovered that my heart for evangelism was so intense that I could not cease preaching the gospel of Christ. Farm responsibilities permitting, I readily accepted opportunities to preach "Jesus Christ and Him crucified." [1] Since Fran's salvation experience at the first barn revival meeting, she, too, has been an energetic evangelist seeking out those who needed Jesus in their lives.

At its inception, Fran and I became the pastors of the interdenominational Christian Fellowship known as The Country Church at Ruthton, MN.

Though not always an easy task, the pastorate has given us many very rewarding opportunities to serve in the Lord's harvest field. Fran's unfailing devotion to this calling is admirable. She has never doubted that God has led the church here in Ruthton and has provided the best path for us to travel. Her faithfulness has been tested and found worthy.

The Church has moved and changed addresses over the years as the number of people attending has continued to grow, causing us to search out bigger facilities. We have had to undertake a church building project on the edge of town to be a lighthouse that will draw many souls into the kingdom. God has been faithful and has

---

[1] 1 Corinthians 2:2

poured His abundant blessings upon us. May the Lord be praised!

If, on a Sunday morning, you are traveling northeastward (or southwestward) across southern Minnesota on Highway 23, stop and visit with us. You will find a friendly welcome awaits you.

Chapter Eleven

Twenty Years Ministering at Barn Revivals
(Contributed by Rev. Henry Vanderbush)

When I think of that first Barn Revival on the Richard DeRuyter farm way back in October of 1984, and consider how the concept has spread, I can do nothing else but praise the Lord, for truly, He gets all the glory. It has now spread to so many states that it seems farmers all over are calling for barn revivals.

Down through the last twenty years, we have held barn revivals in many different settings – machine sheds, sale barns, old-fashioned milking barns, a horse barn, an airplane hangar, haylofts, you name it – we've been there, too. Down in southwestern Minnesota, the services were held in the walk-in haymow while the farmer was milking down below. Swallows were flying in and out, and occasionally a cat would brush by your legs. It's a wonderful place to worship the Lord, preach the Word, and enjoy the presence of God. One farmer and his wife, Rodger and Linda Brandt from Clinton, Minnesota, deserve honorable mention because they have held twenty barn revivals on their farm in the past twenty years. God bless them for their faithfulness, hard work, and perseverance.

Barn revivals have proven to be God's way of cutting across denominational barriers to bring people from all walks of life and religious backgrounds together. It seems that people are honest and open in a barn because they realize they are not being involved with any church or denomination. In a barn setting, people quickly relax and set aside any worries they've encountered during the day. That may be the reason people love to come to a barn revival, for there is nothing required but to relax, obey God, and go with the flow.

I have discovered that when farmers get turned on to God, you cannot stop them. They love their Bibles and take them everywhere. I've seen them on bulk tanks, in machine shops, and always in the cabs of their tractors. They really believe that the cure for everything can be found in the Bible.

I know one farmer who read to his herd of dairy cows and God healed the entire herd of mastitis. Another farmer's fields were being plagued by corn borers, so knowing that Psalm 91 says, "Nor shall any plague come near your dwelling," he walked through his cornfields, read the Bible, claimed the promise and commanded all the corn borers to leave. Every worm left and his field looked like an oasis in the desert.

God, a Farmer & a Bale of Hay

When I sit on a bale of hay with a farmer and he tells me what effect the barn revivals have had on him, I feel like I want to stay right there with my ministry.

The first man God created was the farmer Adam. The word "Adam" means "red earth." Do you know that redemption is the only thing that the earth cannot provide? Everything your eye has looked at since it first opened has been made out of this earth. I have found that the footsteps of a farmer who loves not only his farm and the soil, but also the God who created it is the best fertilizer for the soil. I believe this is the reason God blesses the barn revivals. Redemption started in a barn and it is continuing there today.

To get the concept of barn revivals started, God needed to speak to a farmer: He chose Rich DeRuyter for this project. Although he feared what his neighbors would say and becoming the "laughing stock" of the community, Rich chose to obey God. No wonder God is using him today. He has never tried to make a name for himself. His entire purpose is to lift up Jesus and make His name known. In fact, when I sit and listen to Rich, even in our casual conversation, I feel like I am hearing what Jesus is trying to tell us.

Eternity alone will reveal what affect the barn revivals have had on my life and ministry, but I feel like God is saying to me, "Keep it simple, Henry. That's the way I can use it."

After thirty years of evangelistic ministry, traveling all over the nation and overseas, these last years have been so unique in that they have taken me back to my roots, back to the farm and the upper Midwest. I started my ministry in a barn preaching to Dad's cows, and it looks like I may be ending my ministry preaching in barns! Nothing could make me happier! Thank you, Richard! Thank You God!

Chapter 12

DeRuyter's Gold Nuggets

Privileged beyond measure, I am grateful to the Lord for the journey through life He planned and has been directing for me. My story, a drama illustrating the road from the darkness of sin to the light of God's Word, has been unfolding on the stage of real life. Never in my wildest dreams could I have imagined the pathway I have taken under His guidance.

To me, one thing is crystal clear. God loves His creation. Why the Creator of the universe and everything in it would deal with me on a personal basis is a mystery to me. My path through life is only one of the billions of unique journeys He has prepared; yours, too, is different from all the others.

His love for each one of us is intense and unconditional. Consequently, bringing the greatest possible blessing into our lives is His earnest desire.

Here is another little nugget of DeRuyter wisdom. I cannot relive the past and attempt to alter my history, but because of the many life-changing experiences the Lord has placed on my pathway of life, I can make a better and more productive future. Today is the pivot point between yesterday and tomorrow. Since I'm determined to enjoy today, I'll not attempt to do the things I didn't do yesterday and those things I will do tomorrow. Yesterday and tomorrow are two time zones that do not exist. In Psalm 118:24, the Lord declared, "This is the day the Lord has made ...." I have chosen to rejoice and be glad in it, because it is a gift from God. I will make myself available to be His vessel fit for the Master's use. May I walk humbly with my God and tremble at His Word.

According to my thinking, an altar is simply a place where God and I have down-to-earth but vital communication concerning my walk before Him. I believe there have been three important altars in my journey with God. In my experience, these have occurred in times of great stress.

Firstly, disheartened by the seemingly ceaseless spring rain and the resulting delays in my farming activities, standing ankle deep in muck in my cow yard, I gave my farm to God and told Him to do whatever He wanted with it. At that point in my walk with God, I was willing to give Him possessions, but not myself. It appears that He accepted my gift and used it to bring blessings of a spiritual nature to the area – revival. My altar was a mucky cow yard. He didn't seem concerned about the environment around me; I believe He was searching out the condition of my heart.

God, a Farmer & a Bale of Hay

Secondly, desperately seeking the peace that Jesus said He left here for me, I knelt beside a bale of hay in the loft of my cow barn. There, with a truly repenting heart, I asked God to forgive my sins. I accepted God's great salvation and the peace of mind that accompanied it. Willing to give Him my sin problem, I was not yet ready to give myself, completely. My altar was an ordinary bale of hay. The Holy Spirit came to dwell within me, and at that very significant moment in my life, He commenced the heart surgery, figuratively speaking, that I needed.

Thirdly, with cautious confidence, I stood before the congregation of the Country Church and accepted the request that I become its pastor. My altar was the pulpit. Willing now to give myself completely to the work of the Lord, I was prepared to labor in the harvest field He ordained for me.

DeRuyter's Gold Nuggets

Chapter 13

The Salvation of God

Glossary of important terms found in the following verses of scriptures:

Confess – acknowledge, admit
Eternal – everlasting, never-ending
Glory – magnificence, splendor, beauty, grandeur
Grace – unmerited (undeserved) favor
Justified – just as if you had never sinned, made right before God
Redemption – deliverance, rescue, liberation
Righteousness – moral lifestyle before God
Sin – disobedience to God
Salvation – deliverance, rescue, liberation
Saved – rescued from the curse of sin

Important Scriptures:

"For all have sinned and fall short of the glory of God, being justified freely by His Grace through the redemption that is in Jesus Christ." (Romans 3:23, 24)

When Adam and Eve ate fruit from the tree of the knowledge of good and evil that grew in the middle of the Garden of Eden, sin entered into the world. Having been commanded not to eat fruit from that tree, they sinned when they ate the forbidden fruit. Disobedience to God is sin. In this manner, sin entered into the human race.

"For the wages of sin is death, but the gift of God is eternal life in Christ Jesus our Lord." (Romans 6:23)

Certainly, sin can contribute to an untimely death of a person. However, the word "death" as used here does not mean the immediate death of the physical body. It refers to a separation from God. Sin that has not been forgiven by the Lord will keep a person from relationship with God now and throughout eternity.

"For whoever calls on the name of the Lord shall be saved." (Romans 10:13)

Anyone who has heard the name of Jesus and believes He exists can ask for forgiveness of sins and become a child of God.

"Nor is there salvation in any other, for there is no other name under heaven given among men by which we must be saved." (Acts 4:12)

Salvation is provided through belief in Jesus, the only Son of God, who came to earth, lived a sinless life, and shed his precious blood on the Cross of Calvary to deal with our sin problem. God has so much love for us that He provided the only possible solution to sin.

"If we confess our sins, He is faithful and just to forgive us our sins and to cleanse us from all unrighteousness." (1 John 1:9)

To be cleansed by God from all unrighteousness brings us freedom to talk to God as we would talk to a friend. However, when we have not confessed our sin, it is a barrier between God and ourselves and communication with Him becomes very difficult because of the guilty feeling we have within us.

Here's an illustration: You are walking down a sidewalk in town and you see a friend you have offended in some way coming toward you. A sudden desire to cross to the other side of the street and walk down the sidewalk there overpowers your better judgment and you escape the encounter with your friend.

"For by grace you have been saved through faith, and that not of yourselves; it is the gift of God, not of works, lest anyone should boast." (Ephesians 2:8, 9)

No amount of good works can earn salvation for us. You cannot pay for a gift.

The Salvation of God

"If you confess with your mouth the Lord Jesus and believe in your heart that God has raised Him from the dead, you will be saved. For with the heart one believes unto righteousness, and with the mouth confession is made unto salvation." (Romans 10:9, 10)

Confessing with your mouth is more than a mere thought. It is important to tell others about your decision to follow Jesus Christ. They can help you as you learn to walk the paths of righteousness for Jesus' sake.

If my testimony and this discussion of some Scripture verses have helped you understand God's love for you, your sinful condition that will keep you from an eternity with Jesus in heaven, and your need for a Savior, then, this book will have served its purpose. When you decide to accept Jesus Christ into your life as Savior and Lord, the angels in heaven will rejoice around the throne of God because of your repenting heart and confession of faith in Jesus.

There is no better time than right now to invite Jesus into your heart.[1] No formal prayer is required. Bow your head, close your eyes to keep out distractions, and talk to the Lord. He is now and always has been your best friend.

---

[1] 2 Corinthians 6:2

God, a Farmer & a Bale of Hay

If you have difficulty getting started, then you may use the following prayer:

> **Heavenly Father, I know that You love me unconditionally. I know I have sinned; I am not worthy of salvation; I can't earn it through works. I believe in Jesus and I accept the salvation He provided for me on the Cross. Forgive me the sins I have committed and cleanse me from all unrighteousness. I accept Jesus into my heart and I welcome the Holy Spirit as my comforter, teacher and guide. Teach me Your ways. I want to walk the paths of righteousness for Jesus' sake. Amen**

You have accepted God's gift of eternal life in Christ Jesus. I praise the Lord for your salvation. You are now my brother/sister in the Lord. As a token of our love, I would greatly appreciate a note from you telling me of your salvation – the greatest gift you will ever receive!

Rev. Rich DeRuyter
P.O. Box 100
851 Leo Ave.
Ruthton, Minnesota
USA 56170-5015

The Salvation of God

God, a Farmer & a Bale of Hay

The Salvation of God

Printed in the United States
30418LVS00006B/118-534